When the Wolves Came Back

Matt Reher

Danielle Shusterman

This is a big park.

park →

Wyoming →

2

Yellowstone
National Park
2,219,791 acres

Delaware
1,268,480 acres

3

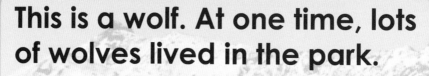

This is a wolf. At one time, lots of wolves lived in the park.

People would kill the wolves to keep their animals safe.

So, for many years, there were no wolves here.

Wolves are the top of their food chain. This means that wolves eat many other animals.

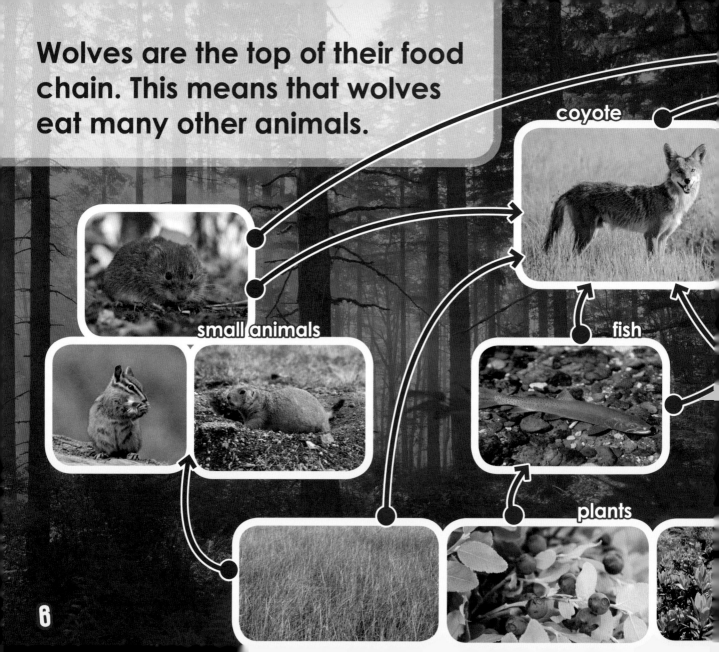

coyote

small animals

fish

plants

wolf

deer

bison

This is how energy flows.

7

bison

With no wolves in this park, there were too many big animals eating plants. They ate all the grass and all the baby trees before they could grow up.

8
elk

bear

Small animals like mice and rabbits had trouble finding food. They began to die out.

osprey

coyote

Even worse, coyotes were catching all the small animals they could. There weren't many left for birds to eat.

9

Many of the park's plants were gone. So were the small animals and birds.

What did the people that help the park do to fix this?

They put wolves back into the park.

First, the wolves ate lots of deer and other big animals. Now there weren't so many big animals eating plants.

The plants started to come back. The grass began to grow taller.

The trees could grow up. In just six years, some trees grew three to five times their size!

5X

14

Now, birds could make nests in these big, beautiful trees.

Beavers need these trees, too. They came back to the park to eat bark from these trees.

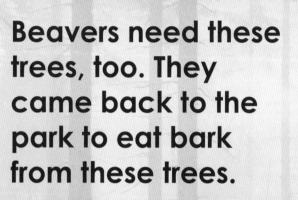

bark

pond

dam

Beavers make dams. Dams stop water and make ponds. Lots of fish and birds came to live in the ponds.

There were more bears in the park, too. They were happy to eat lots of berries from the new plants.

The wolves hunted the coyotes. There were not as many coyotes eating the small animals.

fox

mouse

Now there were more small animals like rabbits and mice in the park.

rabbit

pronghorn

20

With more small animals to eat and trees for nests, big birds like ravens and bald eagles came back.

Wolves didn't always eat all of their food.

coyote

magpie

eagle

bear

They left some meat and skin on the bones for the other animals to eat.

23

Without wolves, we might have lost this park.

Wolves helped fix the park's food chain. Now the park is full of all kinds of plants and animals.

In this park, wolves are the kings and queens.

Afterword

While the loss of wolves from Yellowstone National Park drove the extreme changes in the park's food chain and landscape, placing them back may not be the only factor that has helped the park's recovery. Human efforts, natural events like forest fires, and changes in weather have made a difference as well. The landscape of Yellowstone National Park is ever-changing. The wolves' absence has shaped it for nearly 100 years and their return will help to shape it for the next century and beyond.

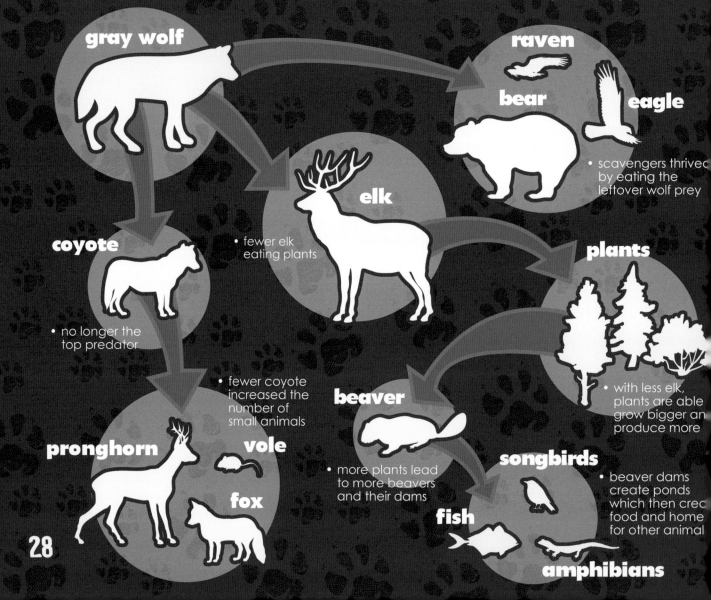

Top Down Cascade

Putting wolves back into Yellowstone National Park affected not just their prey but the entire complex ecosystem.

gray wolf

raven

bear

eagle

- scavengers thrived by eating the leftover wolf prey

elk

- fewer elk eating plants

coyote

- no longer the top predator

plants

- with less elk, plants are able grow bigger an produce more

beaver

- more plants lead to more beavers and their dams

pronghorn

vole

- fewer coyote increased the number of small animals

fox

songbirds

- beaver dams create ponds which then crec food and home for other animal

fish

amphibians

28

Before and After

From 1926-1994, wolves were eliminated from Yellowstone. With the reintroduction of wolves in 1994, the number of animals in the park greatly changed. Below are three examples of the animals affected.

= 100 wolves
= 100 elk
= 100 coyotes
= 1 beaver colony

1926-1994

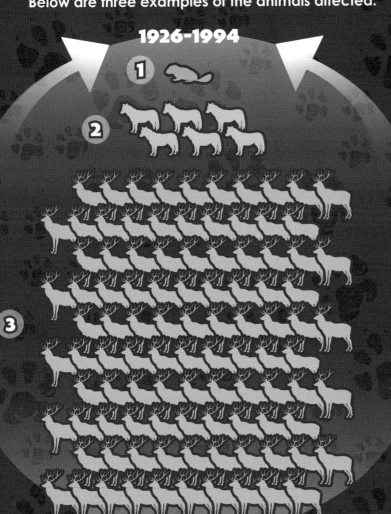

1994-2015

29

Where Gray Wolves Live

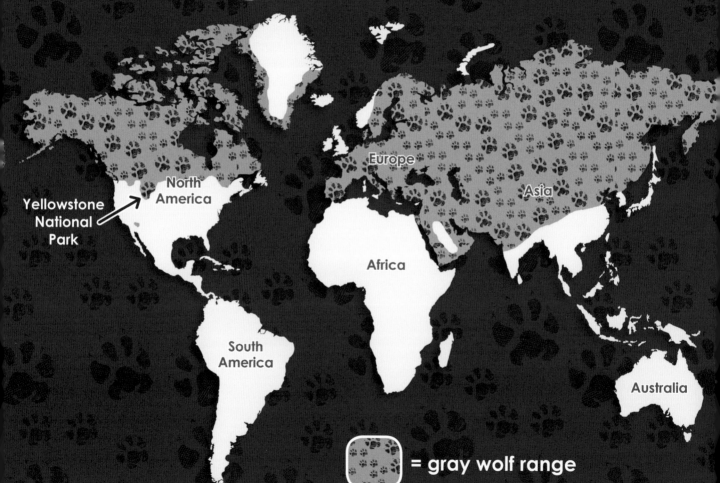

Yellowstone National Park

North America

Europe

Asia

Africa

South America

Australia

= gray wolf range

Use words you *know* to read *new* words!

<u>all</u>	<u>ea</u>t	<u>see</u>
tall	eats	tree
taller	eating	trees
tallest	eagles	three
small	meat	need
smaller	means	keep
smallest	beavers	deer
bald	years	queen
always		

		<u>c</u><u>ar</u>
		bark
	<u>f</u><u>u</u>n	park
	hunt	start
<u>live</u>	hunter	starting
living	hunting	started
lived	hunted	

Inflectional Ending *Practice*

Fill in the blank by matching the word to the sentence.

Wolves _____ fix the park's food chain.　　　taller

There were too many big animals _____ plants.　　　helped

The plants _____ to come back.　　　eating

The grass began to grow _____.　　　started

Tricky Words

beautiful

left

before

began

lost

trouble

gone